By the same author

POETRY

Prometheus Rebound and Other Mythology
Philosophy and Poetry
The Portico Convention
Excavated Athens to Alexandria

ART BOOKS

Monumental Athens Urban

ESSAYS & REVIEWS

Fairy Tale Logic for The Athens Academy
Architecture of Public Policy
In|Sight: African Photographers 1940 to Present
A Substitute for Something Else
Digital Philosophy

EXHIBITIONS

Architect of Public Policy
7th Berlin Biennale

Of Light | A Dialogue with Sol LeWitt
Mass MoCA

A Digital City of Art and Architecture
Manifesta Biennale

THERAPY WITH ANTIGONE
AND THE TRILOGY VERSES

G.F. Zaimis

Spuyten Duyvil
New York City

© 2017 G.F. Zaimis
ISBN 978-1-944682-40-8

Front Cover: Untitled, Mark Rothko, 1968
                  Acrylic on paper mounted on canvas
                  Courtesy Private Collection

Library of Congress Cataloging-in-Publication Data

Names: Zaimis, G. F., author.
Title: Therapy with Antigone and the trilogy verses / G.F. Zaimis.
Description: New York City : Spuyten Duyvil, 2017.
Identifiers: LCCN 2016059110 | ISBN 9781944682408
Classification: LCC PS3626.A62546 A6 2017 | DDC 811/.6--dc23
LC record available at https://lccn.loc.gov/2016059110

for Max

∞

Everything is space and energy.

You become what you think, feel and do.
You are the architect of your reality.

Contents

I. Introduction   ix

II. *Therapy with Antigone*   1
A progression of Sophocles' *Antigone* written as a play in sonnet cycles.
     i.   Invocation
     ii.   Argument
     iii.   Meditation

III. Cleanthes' *Hymn to Zeus*   9
A new translation from Ancient Greek to English verse written in sestina.
     i.   Invocation
     ii.   Argument
     iii.   Prayer

IV. *The Trilogy Verses*   11
Triptychs that pay homage to the Homeric epigram, Haiku and Rothko.

     i.   Semiotics
         All I want   15
         Architecture   16
         Baccarat vase   17
         Blank page   18
         Fear   19
         Gold scarab   20
         Metaphor   21
         Misconception   22
         Misfortune   23
         Poetry   24
         Reading omens   25
         Road signs   26
         Rothko's hand   27
         Surreal   28
         Waiting   29

ii. **Silence**
        Bird cage   33
        Celestial   34
        Collection   35
        Conducive   36
        Holding patterns   37
        Inner worlds   38
        Light hypnotic   39
        Line   40
        Reading silence   41
        Sweet   42
        Synchronicity   43
        Time is   44
        The way out is in   45
        Tria Prima   46
        Unmaking   47
        Why   48

V. **Acknowledgements**

VI. **Author's Biography**

Introduction

The subjects and themes on the forthcoming pages traverse and integrate multiple disciplines from poetry to mythology and philosophy. It is understood that one cannot examine mythology void of philosophy nor the Greek classics less poetry.

Like Clotho's string spun, a trinity of collective meditations are intertwined through literature coupled with a continuum of Heraclitean and Socratic ideologies. We experience these parts of a whole through the eyes of mythology where humanity merges with infinite intelligence, source and the existential dialogue from whence we come, who we are and where we go when we depart from our physical form; the temple of flesh.

Each narrative is didactic in nature and appropriates collective wisdom from ancient Greece as a foundation to translate the essence of being-ness that mirrors the contemporary through myth while logic is seen through the lens of the eternal now being shaped and reshaped.

In the play, *Therapy with Antigone,* the verse meditation progresses Sophocles' classic. Our protagonist, Antigone, serves as a metaphor for humanity and represents moral consciousness reverberated through action and reaction premised upon choices we make through life and how these choices transform our external state of reality which is in essence a mirror reflection of our inner state of being. "As above, so is below", Heraclitus reminds, thus, our inner world mirrors our experiences in our exterior world.

In a lifetime, the soul's journey is a collection of lessons experienced in the physical, material Earth plane. These experiences expand our growth through mindful, awareness and expand our consciousness. These collective experiences are presented to us for review often before or after we transition back to our source.

It is here our heroine, Antigone, is in direct dialogue with her maker. We meet Antigone's soul at the end of Sophocles' version of *Antigone* as she is transitioning from the physical world back to the non-physical. She is in counsel with "the One and All" as Aristotle refers to this source in his *De Anima*. She is in dialogue with her counsellors of light who offer insight, advice to her being. They include Memory, Metatron, the keeper of the collective stream of universal consciousness, and Source.

Memory re-calls, re-counts and re-minds Metatron and Source, who illuminate the sacred universal laws of oneness, correspondence, vibration, polarity, rhythm, cause and effect and gender through her soul's experience and growth during her life in Thebes. Source is omnipresent throughout her journey.

Upon return to the spirit world, her experiences in her earthly life still reverberate heavily as karma has been sewn into her energetic fabric. It is through this cathartic review and journey with her guides, she deleverages; transforms karmic debt through acknowledgment, illumination and forgiveness. She transmutes and heals these energies through conscious awareness prior to spiritual ascension. The story begins in an abstract setting, somewhere in the afterlife in counsel with her advisors.

In the second meditation, Cleanthes' *Hymn to Zeus* presents a new English verse translation from the Ancient Greek. Its original was composed by the Stoic Greek Philosopher. Similar to its prototype though spatially delineated, the poem is pieced into a trinity: Invocation, Argument and Prayer.

However, the poem offers a suggestion that is in contradiction to the foundations of Stoicism. A Stoic need not pray as s/he was known to be in direct dialogue with the gods through one's inner self since reason partakes in divine *logos*. Yet one has the specific impression that Cleanthes was not just writing a poem dedicated to Zeus, the divine, Jove, but rather architecting a prototype or codex to commune directly with the divine which he wanted to record, preserve and distribute through time; timelessness to the everyman, humanity.

Perhaps through this poem Cleanthes came to the understanding that we are in union with the divine source via our thoughts or *divine logos* and because of this so are our feelings and actions in dialogue which reverberate and have the ability to shape and reshape our today for tomorrow. A very progressive idea for an Ancient Greek and Stoic since fate was considered a fixed allotment or apportioned in advance versus the Norse Mythology's version of fate, "wyrd", which was deemed dynamically malleable based upon one's very thoughts, feelings and actions.

Thus, giving even more emphasis to Cleanthes' poem that is considered a *prisca theologia* which integrates almost seamlessly into concepts of perennial philosophies, theology and modern societies who have connected the dots of spirituality through quantum physics and brain science; consciously, mindfully moulding the eternal now through deliberate belief as extensions of source, the "we".

The final series of Triptychs collectively pay homage to the Homeric epigram, the ancient Haiku and Rothko's ideology of three as one which continues to experiment with space and new poetic form through philosophical tones. Layers of words, metaphors, rhyme and meter delineate the "same and other; everything and nothing". They integrate philosophical cannons of Western philosophy and literature that reinforce these principles. All three meditations, *Therapy with Antigone*, *Hymn to Zeus* and *the Trilogy Verses*, remain contemporary yet classic, chastened by English verse written using three poetic forms, the sonnet, sestina and triptych. They serve as creative, literary diplomacy shaped with fragments of reason strung by language and letters.

G.F.Z.

Therapy with Antigone

Therapy with Antigone
A play written in sonnet cycles

CAST

Source
Memory
Metatron
Antigone

Act 1 - Invocation
[Enter] Memory, Antigone and Metatron

[Memory]
You, precious child, defeated—Antigone
By brother's funeral pyre that you aided
While un-abetted, void of sister, Ismene.
You challenged your fate, beyond all odds.

[Antigone]
For longer, the dead I must please—
With them, I shall forever dwell cold
Creon, neither do I support his decrees
Men cannot negate heaven's laws, the gods!

[Metatron]
None are above the One, not even Thebes.
And still, the Moirae are immortal; old.
But if truth be said—you feared god the most,
And alone you died for this noble deed.

Choice stole your youth from the future told.
Death for self-willed pride, became your dose.

Act 2 - Argument
[Enter] Memory, Antigone and Metatron

[Memory]
A holy thing was your deed of loyalty,
Though two vital laws were set; opposed
Yet some who held any authority…
Could brook disobedience imposed.

[Metatron]
For then, you were bound to tragedy
Human law versus divine presupposed.
Creon could not see the hand of god; Antigone
Blinded by arrogance, he unwisely chose.

Free-will versus fate is a person's destiny
Not a predetermined path woven by Atropos—
Rather a balance of choice; reason, said Sophocles
A door to higher consciousness; to be

Though flesh is mortal unlike the cosmos
Similar to threads spun, by life's necessity.

[Antigone]
It feels deep pink; green. Is it you Metatron?
Voices resonate inside as a choir of angelic song
Cleanse my being pure with your spinning cube
Release my betwixt emotions that still pursue

With clockwork motion fuelled by Qi to reveal
I speak my truth once again; help me heal
Through sacred geometry; from the leftover residue
That entangles my soul like water infused

Hear me! I know my devotionals in good faith
Though memory infuses the *air; in octave breaks*

Without resistance; I allow you to brighten
With inner knowledge as healer of the light
Bless me with love, hope in my *fragility zone*
I was not wrong as Creon said—just scared; alone.

I am unlike those *who have double parked*
Life was short; truncated by the King's sharp
Sighted insistence which he thumbed like a harp
Then wielded as a stone behind my back; dark

Can't they see *life doubles back on itself*?
Like two lines that bend into one as they sway
Encircled; again and again to remind ourselves
We are only *particles suspended in the haze*

Like Pythagorean thought, *Algebra of the sky*
I was right to bury my brother, after he died.
I am not lost but feel *your tragedies* as mine
And *your comedies* which we both share
Or *your love stories* and *your dramas* alike

It is said, the fabric we weave is the one we wear

My destiny became like *sliding glass doors*
In and out judgement less the moral thread
While the jury biased in the eyes of the throne
Only to declare pre-emptively, "Off with my head".

Even Alice in Wonderland got a second chance
As she dropped down the rabbit hole, of sorts
Though contrary to popular belief, she did enhance
Many a perspective, among the Queen's court

So now what? That's what I would like to know…
How to release the seeds which have been sown?

Act 3 - Meditation
[Enter] Source and Antigone

[Source]
I am as you are. Present for time; timelessness
Where Memory witnesses in full consciousness
Are lessons in archaeology that build
The what, when, the why—how you will

I want you to know; you are whole
One within two; this is your soul
For it is you dear child; Antigone—
That I comfort now, in all your agony

Releasing the guilt, the fear of delusion
That in clarity; truth, is just an illusion—
Karma which you carry; I now un-weave
This wrath that bleeds; I un-block—delete

The burden that harkens heavy; permeates
Allow the forgiveness to offer a new start

For you are, a radiant child of light
Who beacons, illumines all that is bright
Through the fog; mist of darkness that hears
Or doesn't hear the angels choir always near

Make resolution now, with your higher self
Leave the resentment; anger on the shelf
For Metatron; to remember as royal scribe
Call upon your like-deity; intuition un-blind

Following this guidance as truth; purity
Nous times divine wielding your psyche
Like Aristotle voiced out-loud in *De Anima*
"The One" who first made intellectual capital
The any, the All; I am the mind of the One
Who governs everything; the nothing—the sum

The fabric of the pentacle; reality, the material
Lead to gold as alchemist pulls from the non-physical
Yet allow me to remind, there is always reaction
For even the least; very blip, bling and/or action

Including the silence of muted thought
Or emotions of loss; love over-wrought
Know Antigone that it is you who co-creates
Like the chef who prepares food on the plate
Abundant as the buffet, *all you can eat*

In unison with space, the Demiurge shapes
Moulding the clay of the amphora, the sculptor
Pulling your shape from the mind's vision
Downloaded from source without division
Through the wand of your emotions; the heart
Divine providence; words as directives that I/you impart

In spite of failure which may be, only temporary
You are never alone neither in the momentary
And if there be reason for modification's turn
"We" shall renew like fine print, those concerns.

Open your heart; feel the whole of cosmic reality
It is in affect unique, the structural continuity
And the same with ideas, words that order
Universe governed by its creator; mother, father

Expanding and contracting in rhythm
Full of breath filling each lung with fresh air
While human or creature trumpet their song
In love, hate; peace or war; I am present—here

Like Proclus interpreted Plato's universe…
Two perspectives drawn out that converge.

Note: Words denoted in italic are quoted from Ed Ruscha's painted tapestries.

Hymn to Zeus

Hymn to Zeus
Translated from Cleanthes' 'Hymn to Zeus' in sestina

Invocation

Noblest one, called most powerful ruler; you
Lord of nature, governing all by your divine law; Zeus
"I call upon thee." It is just any and all address, you:
Our origin, design bear likeness to your line as two
5   We live, move as myriad creature, physical on earth
            akin to you

Argument

I sing your praise, this constant rule
Universe whole; spinning 'round your truth
While obeying your beacon call – lead by the hand that rule
With lightened servant in palm, you prove
10   By your electric bolt sounded by thunder through
Jagged sword sent fast, fierce when you brood
Stroked by all and "guided" as energy in space; your
Reason universal that permeates the divine theatre
            directed by you
Mingled from the great, yet twinkled by the minute
            starlight; of you
15   All mighty; your infinite intelligence does sooth
Orchestrated wise from your consciousness, through and through
In divinity, celestial sphere gifted by your oceans imbued
Less the shadow, amidst man's folly who live void of your
            light, to do
Yet still, "you even the uneven" amidst your truth
20   Order the disorder; harmonize the disharmony; it is all dear to you
For it is this whole – your two which is always one
Bending the ends of the line; perfecting eurhythmy
            arranged by you

While darkness flees in your lightness to avoid truth
And the wretched, all wanting, neither sense your cosmic laws;
    their dues

25 As some obey a good life; without understanding
    the essence of you
And others rush with belligerent glory in your shadow, with
    flecks of reflection; hue
Yet some less disciplined intent on your riches, do pursue
Or indulge in carnal pleasures, of your physical flesh that bruise
    pliable bodies taut; attuned
Equivocal of this or that, they desire "your good"

30 Though strive for a cause; as fledglings often do; yet undo
"Cloud-wrapped ruler", omniscient seer; you are all giving
    to us; Zeus

Prayer

Deliver humanity from our ignorance, less we deconstruct
    ourselves, adieu
Allow us to disperse your insight through our souls, anew
To embrace, receive your light while governing juste

35 So we may honor as you have honored us, too
Praising all of you; your divine resonance that prove
From the mortal to immortal; all flecks of you –
You, in reflection of clemency, grace that imbues
And behold your work; universal law as proof.

Note: Cleanthes, the Stoic Philosopher was born at Assos in the Troad, c. 331 B.C. A successor to Zeno, the founder of Stoicism, he embodied a deep reverence for Nature, Destiny, Zeus, Providence, Heavenly bodies and Universal Reason. He revolutionized the study and understanding of physics and matter; energy beyond the material, seeing death as the transformation of the physical body back to the native birthplace "in the heavenlies". The poem is translated from Ancient Greek to English verse.

TRIPTYCHS

SEMIOTICS

All I want

"All I want is TLC when I want it. Your attention when you are busy or talking on the phone."

"Can you change your schedule; your program and come home?"

"All I want is what I want. And all you want is unknown."

Architecture

It's all about light and the use thereof

The reflection of shape; volume and void

Imagery, perception or communication of.

Baccarat vase

It was a tall, I-beam structure, the pellucid crystal vase

Synonymous to the Seagram Building, though art de la table

Beauty's heir in proportion or poems; Baudelaire.

Blank page

It is a white box; long to fill with blocks.

The intangible plot—ideas or thought

Like a blank canvas taut; experiment's lot.

Fear

She came into this world immersed in fear, times two.

It was a part of her fabric that would be solved or resolved to reach the root.

Only to reveal, "it is not better to be frightened than to be uncertain about truth".

Note: Charles Dickens, *A Tale of Two Cities*.

Gold scarab

Your skin gleams of royal blood –

As it glistens of black lacquer; gold

Protector of kings; the written word.

Metaphor

The old, dying dog is a metaphor.

It is clear that this is about much more

Like the scar cut that still bores.

Misconception

I had always thought my maker; she,

Had not understood her pupil, me –

Though years astride after she left, I could see.

Misfortune

As referenced in Plato's *Timaeus*; it was solid infrastructure in place –

Yet the city "beyond the pillars of Heraklion, sank into the ocean"; in emergency, unexpected departure; the worst case…

They recall how, the lawyers, insurance— the brother; lied about the remains of the day.

Poetry

It's all about imagery –

The vehicle of language; photography

In cohesive expression of synergy.

Reading omens

They arrive with the morning light; three fiduciaries intrinsic to time.

Red bird has returned from the past; Salt and Pepper reminds that the present will not last

And the future, near while gazing tender, into her eyes.

Road signs

Someone said, he had her father's lips,
Familiar height from head to hip

And her mother's birthday is yours
As if a window to see the door

Not to mention the hands; and laugh
Or shoe size imprinted like aether's map.

Rothko's hand

Color moves on paper much different than canvas.

Rothko's hand conceived it to sweep the breadth of boundary; lurid intensity bound to fabric post-haste

Like a fraction of a whole, partial truth or absolute vision blurred; erased.

Surreal

Listen to the body language not the words.

The semiotics of signs, language unspoken;
heard

Characterized by fantastic imagery;
philosophy un-blurred.

Waiting

It was for me; you were waiting—

As I approached the church, late

Like Buddha in pose, with meditative state.

SILENCE

Bird cage

We moved our resident parakeet from his jail-bird cage to the Taj Mahal –

The bird's life was plenty as suburbia's shopping mall.

Or was it? It was still captive in a cage after all.

Celestial

She is the brightest star in the sky.

The goddess exalted by the fish with four eyes; unbound into the night.

Sharing love, beauty, art; glorified.

Collection

A collection of precious feelings stade;

Culled as memories from the heart; praised

With emotional gravity of time; weighed.

Conducive

"How long would you suppose synchronicity lasts?"

I suppose it lasts as long as the conductor(s) are conducive...

As long as they are open, synchronous and un-obtrusive.

Holding patterns

Is it you trying to fix
Something—or in reality nix

The past; that you know is done
Reminiscent of; a version of you, gone

Unlike the feeling of one that won't
Let your heart; soul alone

Inner worlds

It was in dialogue we were discussing the abstract, intangible—the essence of the human being.

And the muse said to me, "Isn't life truly about the inner world of feeling?"

It was a pure notion which I, too enamored by the outside noise had not seen.

Light hypnotic

How hypnotic the morning light. In March right before and after the equinox is reborn.

A renaissance of magnificence is the blessings of life as they are given golden rays, despite pagan lore.

Dormant seeds which lay still in soil's flesh; our hearts; offering hope manifest for love after winter's storm.

Line

When it splits, the line

When it parts in two; divides

Then we will see who, stands aside.

Reading silence

There is much to read

Silence is a powerful deed

A catalyst held at stoic stead.

Sweet

He needs something sweet to stave-off the bitterness.

Placate his desire per se like invert's shaped dress—

Satisfy the hunger; the craving for emotional flesh.

Synchronicity

Ideas, numbers, dreams; the union between
an inner existence

With the outer world of tangible experience

Not of, seemingly unrelated coincidence…

Time is

What if time is not linear but rather spatial;

Circular without beginning or end but a constant state of being; parallel

And perhaps time does not pass through us but rather we through it; physical?

The way out is in

1.
The way out is in.

Through the thick of it

Versus around the bend.

2.
Traverse the middle

Less the noise; chatter

Not the physical latter.

3.
Metaphor's nuclei

The heart's eye

From there; you will find

From here; you find
        all that matters.

Tria prima

Principles that give essence and form; mercury to fuse volatility, spirit's imagination, mental facilities that transform

Sulfur, the binding agent, a catalyst for flammability; the soul spread in between, emotions thereof

Like incarnate dye to solidify; the shape physical from salt to fix as flesh and bone.

Unmaking

It can be unmade—
Only where it has been made

It must be taken all the same
From whence it first came

Back to the seat of the soul
The psyche to heal the hole.

Why

The reason precipitated by –

A mind's quest for intellectual query

Is the philosopher's tool; necessary.

Acknowledgements

I acknowledge the intellectual support of the following people who assisted in advocating these ideas; words that have shaped this book. I would like to express my gratitude and appreciation to Tod Thilleman, Publisher, who honorably embraced this manuscript with light; mercurial wings. His work and understanding of mythology and perennial philosophies have facilitated union for my voice to be heard; spoken into an ocean as a ripple of vibration.

Rachel Hadas for her sparkling dialogue full of wisdom; synchronicities that imbue the knowledge of the Classics which inspires, reveals; Elizabeth J. Coleman whose porous ability to translate images, sound, memory into words unveils her expansive consciousness as brails of light on "ocean's burlap weave"; Cecile Margellos at Yale University Press who graciously; elegantly received and advocated my poetic; philosophical voice from inception; Maria Georgopoulou at the Gennadius Library of the American School for Classical Studies, Athens whose expansive vision and grace astutely imbues the contemporarily classic; Paolo Colombo whose vision seamlessly unites the contemporary and literary arts as a maestro calling forth an orchestra of color and resonance like an intricate Seferis poem and last but never least, Lee Slonimsky, poet and "Pythagorean" whose writing and work with the sonnet have brought him into relationship with Ancient Greece beyond time; space.

Special thanks to Maria Protopapa at the Research Centre for Greek Philosophy of the Athens Academy, Evangelos Moutsopoulos, Philosopher of Kairicty and Member of the Athens Academy, Rosemary Donnelly at The Athens Centre and the Private Collections who graciously granted permission for the artwork and my family for their support.

GINGER F. ZAIMIS is an American poet, essayist, thinker, serial creative, word collector and Southerner who specializes in architectural forms.

Her grammatology, lectures and perspectives have been published and presented at centers for contemporary art and literature, biennials, museums and The Athens Academy. Her ability to translate and shape space/energy is seen through the lenses of contemporary modernisms and comparative literature connecting dialogues with language, mythology and philosophy while uniting the arts and sciences.

She is the Literary and Arts Chair for the International Friends of Bibliotheca Alexandrina (Greece), the Library of Alexandria and the author of three poetry collections including *Prometheus Rebound and Other Mythology*, *Excavated Athens to Alexandria,* the co-author of *Philosophy and Poetry*, as well as the architect of the poetic forms, the *Portico* and the *Triptych*.

www.ingramcontent.com/pod-product-compliance
Lightning Source LLC
Chambersburg PA
CBHW021158080526
44588CB00008B/409